LINCOLN'S CHRISTMAS MOUSE

STORY BY DORIS GAINES RAPP, Ph.D.

ILLUSTRATIONS BY TOD PETERSON

This work of fiction is for
all my children, young and older,
who delight my life at Christmas time
and every day of all the years.

LINCOLN'S CHRISTMAS MOUSE
published by Daniel's House Publishing

Text and Illustrations: Copyright 1994 by Doris Gaines Rapp, Ph.D.
Second release 2008 for the Lincoln Bicentennial 2009 and the
recognition of the end of the Civil War in 2011

Printed in the United States of America

ISBN 10:   0-9637200-1-5
ISBN 13:   978-0-9637200-1-6

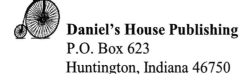 **Daniel's House Publishing**   dorisrapp@yahoo.com
P.O. Box 623
Huntington, Indiana 46750
                              http://dorisrappdanielshousepublishing.blogspot.com

Tod Peterson's illustrations for LINCOLN'S CHRISTMAS MOUSE were selected from those drawn by an illustration class at Bethel College in Mishawaka, Indiana. The class was taught by David Harmon, Assistant Professors of Art.

Hello My name is Hiram P. Antwhistle. The "P" stands for Philadelphia, where I was born. I have lived in the White House for a very long time, even before Mr. Lincoln became president and long after.

Yes, I live in the White House. You see, I am the White House mouse and my wife, Martha, and I live in our little room in the wall near the main stairway leading to Mr. Lincoln's rooms above.

As the appointed White House mouse, I have many responsibilities. Little Willie and Tad Lincoln's yellow mongrel dog, Fido, stayed behind in Springfield, Illinois when their father was elected president. Still, the cook's cat needs considerable exercise, considering all that she eats. And, who would be better suited to provide those calisthenics than I, Hiram P. Antwhistle?

The assignment that has thrilled me the most over my many years in the White House, is the one I fill at Christmas each year. I become the official Christmas mouse.

In 1860, when Mr. Lincoln was elected president of these United States, there was no electricity. And, with no electricity, there were no Christmas programs on television because there was no TV and there were no electronic toys or computer games because they had not yet been invented either. The center of the home at Christmas time in the 1800's was the family's Christmas tree.

Each of the Christmas trees that have stood so tall and fine during my years of White House service has never been made of plastic nor are they decorated with multi-colored blinking lights. They are real pine trees, cut from the forest for the honor of gracing the President's home at this joyous time of year. They have been lit with the glow from carefully placed candles that are balanced on each and every branch.

I have a very important job, you bet. Since the tree is real, it will dry very fast, so it is necessary to make sure that each candle flame has been completely extinguished at the end of the day. The butler snuffs out each candle with a brass candle snuffer. Then, when everyone has gone to bed, I go over the entire tree from star to packages, checking each candle for any small spark or lingering glow. I am sure that I have saved the family more than once from certain fire.

But the
Christmas of 1864
was different.
It was the coldest
winter that anyone
could remember.
Many logs were
needed for each
fireplace and stove.
The Civil War had
lasted a very long time
and Mr. Lincoln wasn't
sure that a tree should
be used just to decorate
the White House.

Perhaps, he felt it would be too extravagant to squander needed
timber on a tree for the hall. But, I had hoped if I could just come
up with a good reason to put up the tree, maybe Mr. Lincoln
would reconsider.

Early one day in December of that year, I found Martha scurrying around under the great dining room table, filling her apron pockets with crumbs and morsels of food. At first, I tried to keep up with her, but she was too fast for me as she darted round and round. I had to rest for a moment on the side of a table leg in order to catch my breath. Still panting, I finally managed to find enough strength to ask, "Martha, now let us think about this. Can you think of something that would convince Mr. Lincoln to put up a Christmas tree this year?"

"Oh Hiram, I don't know," Martha sighed. She was so disappointed about the prospect of not having a tree for the yuletide season. "But wait!" Martha stopped and nibbled on a biscuit crumb

she had stuffed in her pocket. "What if we could find a use for the tree after the holidays? Maybe if he didn't think the tree would be wasted, he'd allow one to be cut for the house." Martha really began to get excited as she thought about the possibility.

"A use for the pine tree?" I felt the spiny softness of my mustache, which I had been twirling between my finger tips, slip from my touch. "But of course! Use the tree later! Well, let's see . . . There's always a need for logs for the fireplace."

"That's true. But, it's not very creative, Hiram," Martha whispered, as her little voice squeaked apologetically.

"Creative? That's an idea. Let's ask Henrietta. She may know." I was beginning to think that perhaps there may be a solution to this situation after all.

Henrietta is the sewing room mouse. Her room is behind the storage cabinet near the treadle machine that the White House seamstress uses. Exposed to beautiful fabrics and colorful threads, Henrietta has developed quite an imaginative flare.

So . . . on

December 10, 1864,

I, Hiram Antwhistle, skimmered up the side of the back stairway, staying close to the wall as a mouse does. I paused at the doorway to the sewing room to make sure that the treadle was pumping. I knew if the seamstress were sewing, she would not notice me as I darted across the floor.

I found Henrietta admiring a bit of blue silk there near the machine. The hum of the treadle and thrust of the needle muffled our voices from the seamstress's ears. I explained our dilemma to Henrietta and then watched as her face started to brighten. "Henrietta, does your expression mean that you may have the answer to our problem already?"

"**A** use for the old Christmas tree once it has been taken down?" Henrietta sparkled. "Yes, I think I may have what you need. I'll have to think this through, however." Henrietta paused, and taking off her spectacles, she cleaned them on a bit of muslin that she had secured when new sheets were stitched for the President's bed.

From the table beside her chair, which was an upturned thimble, upholstered in a bright chintz, she lifted the scrapbook that she had been keeping for many years. "Well now, let me see." Henrietta leafed through the pages of her generous memory book.

"Mr. Lincoln was elected in 1860 and at that time there were 34 states in the Union. On December 20, 1860, South Carolina seceded, they withdrew from their association with the other United States. By the time of Mr. Lincoln's inauguration in March of 1861, there were only 27 states remaining. Six more had withdrawn."

Henrietta turned a page or two and ran her long nails over the sheets as she scanned the large inserts. "The Lincolns' first White House Christmas was saddened by the death of their good friend, Colonel Edward D. Baker in the battle at Ball's Bluff, Virginia. The fighting was very close to Washington, D.C. Poor Mr. Lincoln grieved over each loss, from the North and the South. The Civil War placed a heavy burden on Mr. Lincoln but he was able to find some pleasure in small kindnesses and thoughtful gestures offered to him."

"On Christmas Day 1861, a long package was delivered to the White House. It was wrapped in brown paper and included a small note." Henrietta laid the book down on her lap and closed her eyes for a moment. "I saw the note lying on the table that evening. Mr. Lincoln's  tears had smudged the script, but I could still read its message. I can see the words in my mind."

"Dear President Lincoln,

My son, Robert, was a private with the 2nd Rhode Island. He didn't want to go to fight but he went anyway. He fell at Manassas. The army sent me his things and this small tin drinking cup was with it all. I would like for you to have it, Sir. Robert loved his country very much."

"She didn't sign the note, Hiram. She just tucked it into the cup and put it in the box." Henrietta opened her eyes and a small tear smeared her glasses and trickled down her cheek.

"Where is that tin cup, Henrietta?" I asked, although I wasn't sure of what use I could make of it.

"I don't know, but I'm sure Mr. Lincoln knows where it is." Henrietta smiled.

"**A**nything else in that scrapbook, Henrietta?" I hoped there would be something else, for I didn't see how a tin cup could help get a Christmas tree for the White House.

"Well, now let's look, Hiram." Henrietta turned a few more sheets of the scrapbook. As she turned yet another page, two long, brown strands of thread fell from the leaves of the book. Henrietta gathered them up gently and whispered, "Ah yes, the little black drummer."

"A drummer, Henrietta?" I heard myself questioning softly.

"Yes, Hiram. These strands of thread represent the two drum sticks that came to Mr. Lincoln on Christmas Eve, 1862. Mrs. Lincoln was reading to nine-year-old Tad. Willie had died in February, when he was eleven, and Mrs. Lincoln doted on little Tad. I remember, the butler came into the room carrying a long package, wrapped in a soft rag cloth. Mr. Lincoln opened the coarsely woven fabric to reveal two worn, palm-darkened drum sticks and a delicately written letter."

"Dear A. Lincoln,

Esther, my cook, former slave, and old friend, asked me to pen this letter to you at Christmas time, 1862. She does not read nor write. Her young son, Benjamin, was a drummer boy, excused from the 79th U.S. Colored Troops for a week because of his mother's failing health. As he made his way home on December 11, he was walking near Fredericksburg, Virginia when the Union forces began shelling the town. Esther would like for you to have Benjamin's drum sticks. She said to tell you that there is still a lot of music left in them.

Sincerely,

Mrs. Paul Anderson"

"Drum sticks, Henrietta? But, Henrietta, I still don't understand." I sat, puzzled, on the pillow made of downy feathers and covered with drapery fabric from the East Room.

"Yes, drum sticks, Hiram. And, I think I'm beginning to get the thread of an idea. Now let me see . . . " Henrietta fanned the pages rapidly, for this time she knew what she was looking for.

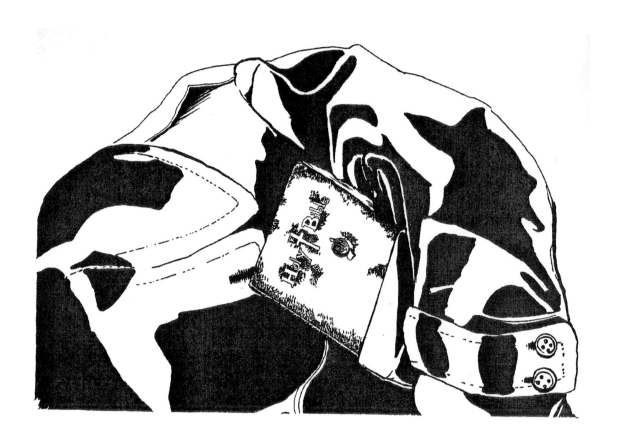

"Yes, yes, here it is. Christmas, 1863 followed on the heals of many battles, Chickamauga, Chattanooga, then Missionary Ridge.

A young Rebel Lieutenant was encamped on the top of Missionary Ridge, when General Phil Sheridan and his men started up the hill and opened fire. The Confederate Lieutenant was struck in the chest and fell. He was taken to a Union hospital where he was treated. His physician sent Mr. Lincoln the musket ball that had struck the young officer, still buried in the Bible the Lieutenant always carried inside his jacket." Henrietta patted the page of her scrapbook. "Yes, right here, a scrap from the newspaper in which the Bible had been wrapped."

"Henrietta! A tin cup, two drum sticks, and a Bible with a bullet imbedded in its middle. I don't understand at all." I scratched my head and rolled my eyes. "How does that help us get a Christmas tree here in 1864?"

"Get up early and bring Martha back here just before dawn, while the house is still asleep." Henrietta jumped to her feet and shoved me back down the stairs. Then she went to work gathering the items she would need.

While the seamstress stitched another seam, Henrietta darted into the closet where patterns were stored. From a stock of pattern paper, Henrietta scratched at the stack until a single sheet fell to the floor. Henrietta pushed it under the hanging dress that the seamstress had been making for Mrs. Lincoln so the sewing lady would not see where it had fallen.

Next, Henrietta studied the room. Then, she waited for the safest moment. At last, she skimmed across the floor to where a bit of charcoal had fallen when the embers were removed from the fireplace. She selected a piece that she could carry and drew it into the closet, depositing it with the tracing paper.

There, in the fabric closet, she worked. Only the little light that streamed in through the small opening left in the door guided her work.

Suddenly, she heard the scratch of a chair on the wooden floor and the clunk of footsteps as the seamstress neared the closet door. Henrietta gasped as she thought of being trapped in the closet, making it difficult for Martha and Hiram to find her in the morning.

Luckily, Henrietta spotted a spool of white thread on the floor near the door. She quickly forced it into the opening just as the seamstress gave the door a gentle push. Thankfully, the seamstress was in too big a hurry to see that the door didn't latch as she turned and hurried down the back stairway. Henrietta sighed deeply, then went back to her work.

"Henrietta?"

I whispered softly, many hours later, as Martha and I entered the sewing room before the sun had risen. The room was still quite dark.

"In here, Hiram and Martha. Come in here," Henrietta requested, as she pulled the paper from under the clothing. "We can't waste any time."

Martha and I helped Henrietta roll up a large white sheet of paper, even though we couldn't see what was drawn on it. Whatever it was, we trusted Henrietta and knew that her plan would work. You bet.

We rolled the paper like a tube. I held up the front end, Henrietta took the middle, and Martha balanced the back on her shoulder. Together, we made our way down the back staircase to Mr. Lincoln's room.

The house was still quite quiet when we entered the bedroom and inched along to the chair that sat beside a small table. Mr. Lincoln's shoe lay on its side beside the chair, so we used it for the first step. Up over the shoe, onto the chair, up the chair ladder back, and onto the table we carried Henrietta's drawing.

Once we reached the table top, we unscrolled the picture and laid it out smoothly on the table's surface. Martha straightened the top part and Henrietta and I took the bottom of the page.

Mr. Lincoln was just beginning to stir when we finished and started down the ladder back chair. Once firmly on the ground, we darted quickly behind the draperies that hung at the windows. We were anxious to see how the illustration would be received.

Mr. Lincoln yawned and stretched and sat for a moment on the side of the long bed. As the morning sun lightened the room his eye caught sight of the white drawing paper, for it had not been there when he had sat in the chair the evening before to remove his shoes.

Mr. Lincoln lifted the paper from the table and took it to the window to study its contents. Martha, Henrietta, and I held our breaths and pulled in our stomachs so as not to be seen.

We watched with anticipation. Slowly, we began to see a warm smile cross Mr. Lincoln's face and spread out between his beard and mustache.

"What is it?" Mrs. Lincoln questioned as she saw the expression of delight on her husband's face. It had been a long time since she had seen him smile.

"Mother, we <u>will</u> have a Christmas tree this year, just like before." Mr. Lincoln dropped the page and embraced his wife.

The paper fell to the floor where Martha and I could see what we had born on our shoulders from the attic into Mr. Lincoln's room. There was the drawing of a Christmas tree and beside the tree, a small table with objects on it. I could not identify each item quickly enough before Mr. Lincoln bent to show the picture to Mrs. Lincoln.

The 1864 holidays were a mixture of joy and sorrow as the fierce Civil War rolled on. Our beautiful country was torn apart by this struggle. But inside the White House, the Christmas tree, lighted by the sparkle of all those candles, seemed to bring Mr. Lincoln new hope.

Before the season was over, while the wreath still hung on the door, a new sound was heard coming from behind the white mansion. The old rail splitter, Abe himself, was found one morning, separating the long pine trunk of the Christmas tree into several rough boards.

Once finished, he gathered them under his long arms and carried them into the tool shed. No one was permitted entry but we all heard the distinct sounds of a saw, and a hammer, and sand paper caressing the timber.

A few days later, as Martha and I warmed ourselves in the sun below the window sill, Mr. Lincoln came in with an object draped with an old blanket. It had been bitter cold and he had worked well into the afternoon. He threw his coat over a chair to reveal rolled up sleeves and an open collar, all covered by a vest that was now missing one button.

"Are they here, Mother?" Mr. Lincoln asked his wife.

"Yes, they are in the box there on the chair." Mrs. Lincoln pointed to the objects she had brought from Mr. Lincoln's desk.

Mr. Lincoln cleared a spot near the window and placed the blanket covered thing in the light that it offered. Carefully, he removed the cover and then we saw it.

There, in the gleaming sunlight stood a small pine table, all polished and smooth, yet rough and handsome.

With great reverence, Mr. Lincoln placed upon the table the objects from his box - a pressed white rag all newly hemmed and embroidered with white doves and edged in lace. He lovingly spread the rag-doily on the crude table. On the cloth, he placed a tin cup filled with candle wax which supported a sturdy wick. Beside the cup-candle he placed a small black Bible, its middle drilled with the ball of a musket, the deadly lead still lodged deeply within the sacred pages. And, with a bit of twine, he fashioned a cross from the two drum sticks and held them erect by placing them in a little groove he had carved in the table top just for that purpose.

I could see tears in Mr. Lincoln's eyes as he held Mrs. Lincoln's hand and they bowed their heads. For, at last, they lay there together, on an alter carved from the tree of peace, in the season of the year when peace was brought to earth, the mementos of three heroes - a Union private, a Confederate officer, and an innocent young black drummer.

.

Historic facts were taken from:

Ward, Geoffrey C. (1990). <u>The Civil War</u> - An Illustrated History. Alfred A.
Knopf, New York.

ABOUT THE AUTHOR

DORIS GAINES RAPP, Ph.D. is a licensed psychologist and writer. She has directed the counseling centers at Bethel College, in Mishawaka and Taylor University, in Upland, Indiana. As a therapist and former teacher, she knows that stories can teach many concepts on many levels. LINCOLN'S CHRISTMAS MOUSE tells an entertaining Christmas story while bringing together elements of our culture which have formerly been divided. Doris Rapp is an author of several other books. Go to: www.dorisgainesrappdanielshousepublishing.blogspot.com and www.prayertherayrapp.blogspot.com for more information. She and her husband, Bill, have six children. Their older four children are grown and have families of their own. Doris and Bill are now rearing their second family, two girls, Kathleen, now 21 and Amanda, now 20. They all wish you a Merry Christmas and pray that it may be a time of healing for us all.

ABOUT THE ARTIST

Tod Peterson was a student at Bethel College in Mishawaka, Indiana, majoring in Visual Communications. While taking an illustration class at Bethel, taught by David Harmon, he entered into a project for developing the drawings for LINCOLN'S CHRISTMAS MOUSE. From the initial drawings, submitted independently by the class members, Tod's were selected and purchased for publication. We hope that you will be as delighted by Tod's creativity and talent as we are.

TO ORDER ADDITIONAL BOOKS

Go to www.dorisgainesrappdanielshousepublishing.blogspot.com or contact Doris Gaines Rapp and Daniel's House Publishing at dorisrappdanielshousepublishing@yahoo.com and order additional books at $19.99 each, PLUS SHIPPING & HANDLING. You may want to log on to Dr. Rapp's Prayer Therapy blog at www.prayertherapyrapp.blogspot.com. You can also reach Doris Gaines Rapp at P.O. Box 623, Huntington, Indiana 46750.